✱ The ✱
HATTERS

A Puritan hat of the 1600's

COLONIAL AMERICAN CRAFTSMEN

The

HATTERS

WRITTEN & ILLUSTRATED BY

Leonard Everett Fisher

FRANKLIN WATTS, INC.

575 Lexington Avenue, New York, N. Y. 10022

For Ruth and Hy

SBN 531–01029–5

Library of Congress Catalog Card Number: 65-21629
© *Copyright 1965 by Leonard Everett Fisher*
Printed in the United States of America

Colonial Americans

THE CABINETMAKERS

THE GLASSMAKERS

THE HATTERS

THE PAPERMAKERS

THE PRINTERS

THE SCHOOLMASTERS

THE SHOEMAKERS

THE SILVERSMITHS

THE TANNERS

THE WEAVERS

THE WIGMAKERS

A Short History

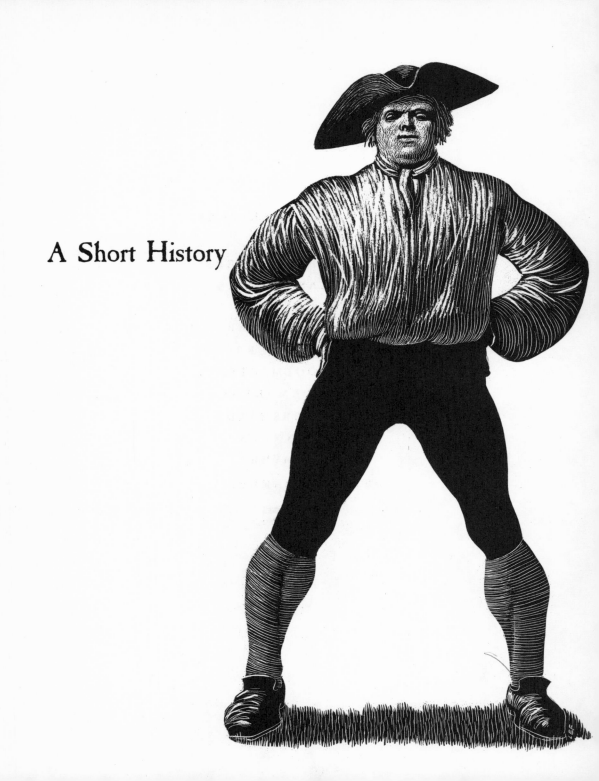

H ATS WERE AMONG THE EARLIEST American products to make England realize the growing power of her colonies. By the early 1730's, American hatters were making about ten thousand hats a year, and were selling them wherever English hatters had customers. Moreover, the American hatters were becoming rich at the expense of English hatmakers. Like everyone else in the British American colonies, the hatters were getting to be a meddlesome lot, from the English point of view.

The London hatters were losing so many customers to their American cousins that they raised a howl of protest. They complained so loudly that on January 13, 1731, the British Parliament passed a law prohibiting "hats or felts, dyed or undyed, finished or unfinished, to be exported from a British Plantation under penalty of fine." This law was called the Hat Act. No one in America paid the slightest attention to it.

In the following year, George II, King of England, issued a public proclamation in which he said that the Hat Act was "an Act to prevent the Exportation of Hats out of any of His Majesty's

☼ 7 ☼

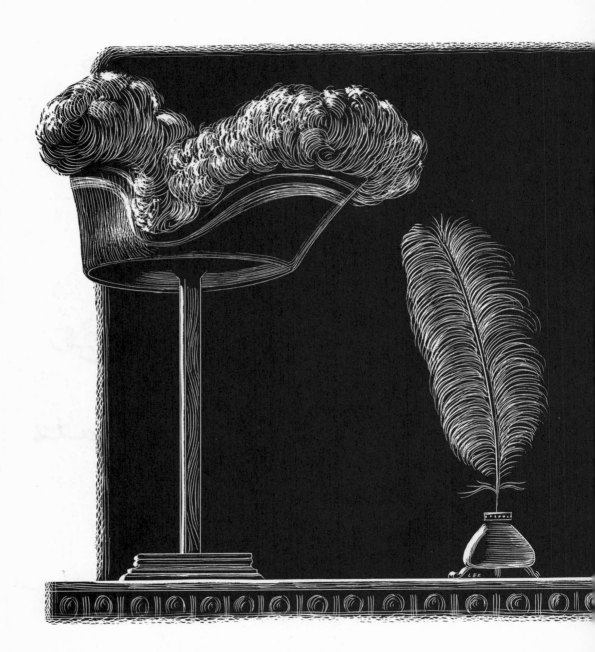

King George II of *England*

Colonies or Plantations in *America,* and to re-
strain the Number of Apprentices taken by the
Hat-makers in the said Colonies or Plantations,
and for the better encouraging the making Hats
in *Great Britain.*"

The *HISTORY*

The Hat Act was only one of the many annoy-
ing laws that drove the people of the colonies to
seek their liberty from English rule forty-five
years later. The events that caused Parliament
to act against the colonial American hatters had
begun more than a hundred years earlier, however.

It all started when the first adventurous set-
tlers reached the shores of North America. There
were abundant raw materials to be found in this
vast, uncivilized land. This was one of the important reasons why England and some of the
other great European powers decided to found
colonies in the New World. The country that
could get the raw materials, turn them into useful products, and sell them at a large profit would
become rich and powerful. Chief among the materials to be found were the skins of fur-bearing
animals — especially the skin of the beaver. At
that time, beaver fur was highly prized for the
making of hats.

The *HISTORY*

In 1606, King James I granted separate charters to two groups of Englishmen, one called the London Company and the other called the Plymouth Company, to set up colonies in a large section of North America called Virginia. One year later, the London Company founded Jamestown, but the Plymouth Company had no such success.

In 1620 the Plymouth Company was renamed the Council for New England, and received a new charter that granted it lands north of Virginia. In that same year the Pilgrims received permission from the London Company to settle in Virginia. Their ship, the *Mayflower,* ran into bad weather, however, and landed on the coast of what is now Massachusetts, on territory granted to the Council for New England. There the Pilgrims established the second permanent English colony in the New World, and named it Plymouth.

Within a short time after the founding of Jamestown and Plymouth, the colonists began to collect furs, sending some of them back to England. When the *Mayflower* first departed from Plymouth on April 5, 1621, she carried in

her hold two hogsheads, or large barrels, of beaver skins. By 1634 the Pilgrims had increased their shipment of beaver skins to twenty hogsheads.

The *HISTORY*

In the meantime, the Dutch had no intention of being left out of the fur trade. In 1609, Henry Hudson, in the service of the Dutch East India Company, had sailed up the graceful river that still bears his name. Soon Dutch traders began to arrive in the area. Finally, in 1621, the Dutch government chartered the Dutch West India Company to establish trading posts as permanent settlements and to colonize the Province of New Netherlands. This was the same land claimed earlier by England.

In 1624 the Dutch company built fur-trading posts at Fort Orange, now Albany, New York, on the Hudson River; and at Fort Nassau on the Delaware River. Some Dutch were also settled at a fort in New York Harbor. In 1625, New Amsterdam was founded on the tip of Manhattan Island, now part of New York City. Later, Fort Good Hope on the Connecticut River was built.

At these and other settlements the Dutch eagerly traded knives, beads, and rum with the

·H·H·

LEF

✿15✿

For a while the Dutch
carried on active fur trading
with the Indians

The *HISTORY*

Indian trappers for beaver skins. The Dutch traders were so good at their work that in the first year of settlement they shipped more than one thousand beaver skins back to Holland. In 1657 they shipped about forty thousand skins from Fort Orange to New Amsterdam. They had taken over a large piece of the fur trade and were making the most of it. But not for long.

The English had allowed the Dutch a somewhat free hand, partly because during some of this time they were engaged in a war with France and Spain, and did not want the strong Dutch people as an enemy, too. The Dutch, meanwhile, were so busy collecting valuable skins that they could not bother to grow the food they needed. Their greed for skins was too great. By 1660 so many beavers had been killed that the Dutch fell to arguing and scheming about the small supply that was left. They did not know the ways of surviving in a wilderness as well as the English did, and England knew it.

Little by little, the power in the colonies — and with it the fur trade — was passing to England. France had in the meantime built an important fur-trading business farther north. New and hardy English colonies began to dot the east-

*In 1664, Peter Stuyvesant,
acting for the Dutch, surrendered
New Netherlands to the English*

ern shoreline. It was only a matter of time before the weakened Dutch would be forced to give up their holdings to England. That event finally happened in 1664, when the Dutch surrendered their Province of New Netherlands, including New Amsterdam, to a British force.

The HISTORY

Unlike the Dutch, the English colonists did not send all their furs back to the mother country. They kept some to make products for themselves, or hats to be sold elsewhere.

In 1662 the Virginia Assembly offered ten pounds of tobacco for every good wool or fur hat produced in Virginia. Only ten years later a group of Massachusetts hatters asked the General Court to cut down on exporting furs, for fear the colonial hatters would have none left for making hats. The Court refused to do this, claiming that colonial hatters made terrible hats that were too expensive; they should at least improve their product and cut down on their price before they asked for government protection. A short time later, the exporting of certain furs other than beaver was stopped.

There was a great demand for hats, both in Europe and the New World. Some men owned great collections of hats, and changed their head-

gear daily. The colonial hatters, as well as other craftsmen, businessmen, and political leaders, knew that if they could turn their raw materials into useful products and sell them at a profit, they would prosper and gain power. That is exactly what they began to do when England tried to stop them with the Hat Act, and failed.

All over the colonies, hats were being made from a variety of animal furs. Most of the hats, however, were made in the areas where the fur trade was greatest, as in New England, New York, New Jersey, and Pennsylvania. At the time the War for Independence from Great Britain began, a center of hatmaking was being established in Connecticut. There the numerous rivers, streams, creeks, and forests attracted fur-bearing animals. And there, in the town of Danbury — which had been founded in 1684 by eight South Norwalk families, one member of whom was a hatter — the story of the colonial American hatter comes to an end. There, as in other early hatmaking centers, the story of the American hatter who was free to do business as he pleased begins. It was in Danbury, in 1780 when the British were all but defeated, that Zadoc Benedict, with one journeyman and two

apprentices, opened a hatmaking factory and prospered. From that time to the years shortly after World War II, Danbury was a leading hat-producing center in the United States. It became known as the Hat City.

The HISTORY

A hat played one unusual role in the cause of American liberty. The King's soldiers, ridiculing the untrained American fighting men, sang a song that compared them to the foppish London dandies of the time, who were called "macaronis."

> *Yankee Doodle went to town*
> *A-riding on a pony,*
> *He stuck a feather in his hat*
> *And called it Macaroni.*

The Americans only laughed, however, and adopted the song as their own. They sang it, and whistled it, and played it on their fifes so often that before long the British never wanted to hear it again. But the Americans never stopped. Just to remind the King's men once more that it was the "macaronis" who had finally won the war, the bands of the Continental Army struck up "Yankee Doodle" on the fields of Yorktown on October 19, 1781, as the defeated British passed in surrender before them. ᔓ

How the
Hatters Worked

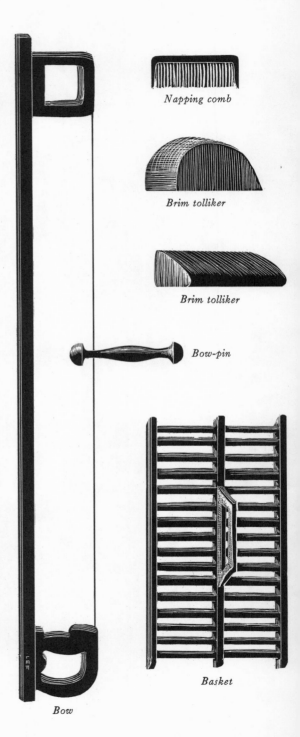

Napping comb

Brim tolliker

Brim tolliker

Bow-pin

Runner-down stick

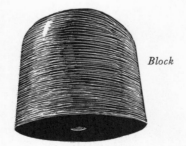

Block

Bottom board

Bow

Basket

IN THE COLONIES NEARLY EVERYONE WORE some kind of headgear. Men and women alike covered their heads with a variety of materials in countless shapes. Mostly they used wool, cotton, straw, and animal fur, though not all these coverings were hats. A hat was considered to be a headdress with a rim or brim all the way round. The best hats were made of beaver fur, because it usually lasted a lifetime. Some men, before they died, even willed their beaver hats to their heirs.

Like the women of today, the colonial women took great delight in wearing fashionable and picturesque, but sometimes impractical, headgear. They appeared in almost everything imaginable: simple cloth caps and ordinary hoods; delicate skullcaps, or cauls; small lacy caps called coifs; large, loose, lacy cornets; mobcaps and nightcaps; bonnets and veils; cross cloths and chin clouts, to mention only a few. None of these were considered to be hats, however, for they were without brims. They were either fashioned by the wearer herself or by a milliner — a maker of headgear for women.

The colonial women did wear hats on occasion,

The *TECHNIQUE*

A hatter's factory of the 1700's

but not nearly as often as the men did. The men's hats were made for them by craftsmen called *hatters*.

From the beginning of colonial rule at Jamestown to the end of it at Yorktown, America's men wore different types of caps and hats. The most popular cap was the Monmouth. Knitted of wool, it fit snugly around the head, just above the ears. Its high, rounded top usually flopped over one ear.

The hats, all handmade, ranged from the dashing, wide-brimmed cavalier or Van Dyke — with or without a gay ostrich feather — to the three-cornered cocked hat or tricorne, with its upturned brim. Whatever the style of hat, the method of manufacture does not seem to have changed much over the colonial years.

The hatmaking craft became an important industry in Europe during the fifteenth century. At that time, felt hats became fashionable. Felt is a thick cloth made of wool or animal fur matted together without weaving or spinning. The method of making the material is called *felting*. Felt can be easily shaped into various forms. Because it is easily shaped, it is an especially good material to use in fashioning a hat.

The *TECHNIQUE*

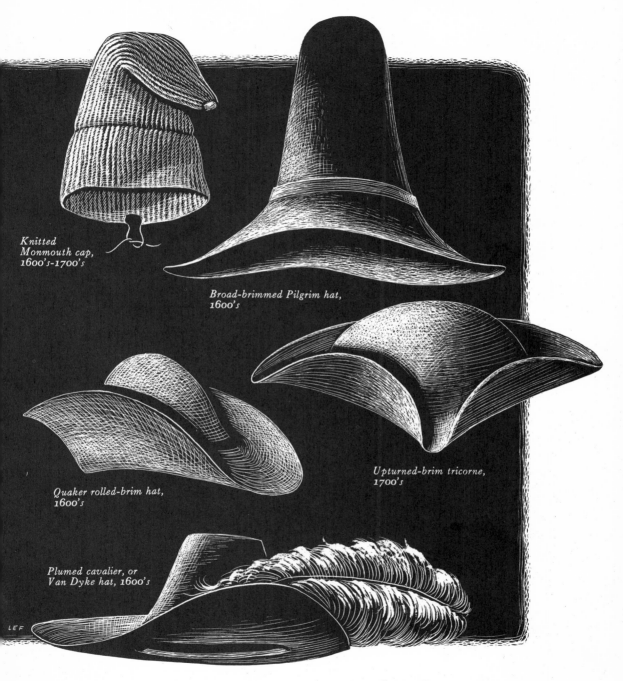

Knitted
Monmouth cap,
1600's-1700's

Broad-brimmed Pilgrim hat,
1600's

Upturned-brim tricorne,
1700's

Quaker rolled-brim hat,
1600's

Plumed cavalier, or
Van Dyke hat, 1600's

LEF

✺ 29 ✺

The *TECHNIQUE*

Beaver fur made felt of the highest excellence. Like most animal fur, it has two layers, or coats. The beaver's outside coat is made up of long, rough, shiny hair, brownish in color. Its undercoat is made of soft, thick hair, bluish in color. The hairs of the outside coat, now called the guard coat, were once called the wind hairs because they were a protection against the cold wind, and fell out during the summer months. The undercoat was called the underfur. It was this underfur that was used to make felt for hats.

Before the hatter could use the underfur, it had to be treated, together with the beaver's skin, in order to preserve it and make it mat better.

When the beaver's furry skin had been removed by the trapper, it was dried. The dried skin, called a *plew* or a pelt, was then treated — cured and tanned — in any one of a number of different ways, to keep it from rotting. Once the pelt had been treated, the wind hair was plucked from it, and the remaining underfur was scraped off. This step was called *currying* the skin. Curing, tanning, and currying the beaver pelts were usually the work of a craftsman called a tanner.

The early hatters knew that the best felt

The TECHNIQUE

seemed to come from old, battered, greasy skins. Most of these skins were supplied by Indian trappers, who tanned them by pounding animal fat, liver, and brains into them: they would then be that much more dirty, greasy, and battered.

Strange as it may seem, many a colonial hatter had to wait until an American beaver fur had been well worn out in Russia before it was returned to his country for him to use. The fur of the American beaver was highly prized in the cold Russian winters because of its shiny wind hairs. Since the wind hairs were of no value to the hatmaker, the fur traders often sold their new skins to the Russians, who used them to line or edge their clothing. After a while, the wind hairs fell out. When that happened, the Russians sold the used furs back to the American traders, who in turn sold them to the eager hatters.

In any event, once the hatter had the underfur scraped from the skin, he was ready to make a *castor,* a beaver hat.

First, the loose fur was washed and combed, or *carded,* to untangle the soggy mass. The carded hair was then allowed to dry. The clean, dry fur next was placed in a pile on a special

❀33❀

The bower,
standing at the hurdle,
snapped the bow

bench called a *hurdle,* where a craftsman known as a *bower* worked.

The hurdle was enclosed in a closet-like room, which was open at the front. A window at the back allowed plenty of working light. Hanging by a cord attached to the ceiling over the hurdle was a *bow*. The bow was a long wooden pole tightly strung with twisted strands of tough catgut. It looked like a huge violin bow.

Standing before his bench, the bower held the bow so that the catgut string touched the loose fur. He then snapped the string with a *bow-pin*. The snapping string scattered the pile of fur, causing it to spread out in a flat oval shape. Each oval of bowed fur was called a *batt*. Each batt was used to make one hat.

The batt was covered with a wet linen cloth while the hatter pressed down on it with a wooden tool called a *basket*. This pressure caused the damp hairs under the cloth to mat, or cling together. When the hairs were well matted, the hatter removed the wet cloth. What once was loose fur was now *felt*.

Next, the hatter placed a triangle-shaped paper on the batt. He folded the batt around the paper. A wet cloth was placed over the now

The TECHNIQUE

folded batt, and once more the hatter pressed the batt, joining the folded edges into one solid piece. All these steps together were called *hardening*.

The hatter next wrapped the hardened batt in the wet cloth and rolled it. Then he unrolled the batt and removed the damp cloth and triangular paper. Now he had a cone-shaped cap called a *body*. The paper had kept the sides of the body from sticking together during the pressing.

Before going on to the next step, the hatter boiled the body in a water-filled, straw-lined vat for about seven hours. This shrank the fur and caused the hairs to cling together even better.

For the following four or five hours the body was kept boiling and wet while the hatter continued to work on it. During this time he stood at a *battery,* which was made of a number of wooden shelves, or *planks,* connected to a kettle that fitted over a brick fireplace. Here the hot and soggy body was repeatedly dipped in the kettle, then rolled and worked over on the plank. Knotted hairs and impurities were removed. The hatter added more fur where it was needed, by patting it into the body with a wet brush. This

The *TECHNIQUE*

Hat bodies

process was called *stopping*. The constant dipping and wetting shrank the body to about one-half its original size. It also made the felt much stronger and thicker than it had been when the fur was first matted.

The TECHNIQUE

Next, the hatter patted soft, short beaver hairs, or *nap*, all over the body with a wet brush. He then placed the body on a rough horsehair cloth and *rolled it off*. That is, he dipped and rolled the body again in order to thoroughly mesh all the hairs that had been patted onto it. All these steps together were called *planking* and *fulling*.

The body was then dried, and those hairs that did not lie flat were cut off with a sharp shaving knife. With that done, the hatter turned up the edge of the body and pushed the top of it down, forming a ringlike fold. He continued to push the top up and down until the body was a flat circle of ringlike folds, one within the other. The flat body with its circular folds was wetted again. The hatter then pressed smooth the center folds until they were equal in measurement to the crown of the hat. He placed the body on a wooden mold, or *block*, and tightly tied a string around the top of the body.

Circular folded body

✸39✸

The *TECHNIQUE*

Using a *runner-down stick,* the hatter worked the string down the sides of the body, firmly pressing it to the block. The block was the same size and shape as the hat crown would be when it was finished. By working and wetting the body, the hatter molded it closely to the block. He then smoothed the body with a wood or bone tool that was shaped to fit the curve of the block.

The part of the body that hung loosely from the bottom of the block was used to make the brim. The hatter flattened the wrinkled brim by placing the blocked body on a flat board, or *bottom board,* and smoothing the brim out with a wooden tool called a *brim tolliker.* He then pressed some of the water out of the newly formed hat with a *stamper.* He raised the nap with a *napping comb.* He carefully cut off the hair tips, and placed the hat in an oven to dry. Once dried, the hat was removed from the mold and dipped into a dye of whatever color was wanted. Next the hat was stiffened.

None of the felt hats worn during colonial times were soft. All of them were stiff. To stiffen a newly made felt, the hatter brushed it with a coat of shellac or glue. Usually he made the shellac and the glue himself.

Runner-down stick

String

Block

1. Working the string down the body

Smoothing tool

Block

2. Smoothing the body

Brim tolliker

Bottom board

3. Smoothing the brim

Napping comb

Bottom board

4. Raising the nap

The *TECHNIQUE*

He made the shellac by mixing a liquid of alcohol and lac. Lac is a sticky material left by insects on the branches of certain Asian trees. It was imported into the colonies in flakes or sheets, which the hatter dissolved in alcohol. He made the glue by soaking the crushed bones, hooves, and hides of animals in warm water.

No matter what liquid was used, the hat lost its shape during the stiffening process. It had to be put in a steam box, where it was again softened. Then it was put back on the block, reshaped, and ironed. After the hat was ironed and became stiff again, it was *pounced with pumice* — rubbed with a powdered stone called pumice — to make it smooth. This ironing and smoothing was called *finishing* the hat.

The hatter next turned his attention to the brim. He either left it alone, cut it down with a sharp knife, or softened it with steam in order to curve it with his curling tools. Once the brim was curled into shape, it was dried and became stiff again. Pumice was once more used to make it smooth.

When the hat had been finished, a thin leather band was sewed to the inside bottom of the crown. The hat was then *dressed,* or decorated.

The *TECHNIQUE*

Sometimes a leather band was added to the outside bottom of the crown. At other times a silk ribbon was sewed around the edge of the brim. Feathers of every shape and description were used as decorations. Cockades, or flower-shaped knots of ribbon, were pinned to some hats.

With one neat final touch the hat was softly brushed. It had been made in America and was worn with a lifetime of pride in its craftsmanship.

Hatters' Terms

BASKET — A wooden tool used in pressing a wet cloth onto the batt.

BATT — A flat oval shape of fur — the material for one hat.

BATTERY — An arrangement of shelves, or planks, around a kettle fitted over a brick fireplace. Here the hat body was boiled and shrunk.

BLOCK — The wooden mold on which the crown of a hat was shaped.

BODY — The cone-shaped cap from which a hat was made.

BOTTOM BOARD — The flat board on which the brim of a hat was formed.

BOW — A tool resembling a huge violin bow. When properly snapped, the bow caused the fur to spread out in the flat oval shape called a batt.

BOWER — The craftsman who worked with a bow, and formed the batts.

BOW-PIN — The tool used by the bower in snapping the bow.

BRIM TOLLIKER — The wooden tool used for smoothing the brim.

CARDING — Combing the wet mass of fur after it had been washed — the first step in making a beaver hat.

CASTOR — A beaver hat.

CURRYING — Scraping the underfur from a pelt.

DRESSING — Decorating a newly finished hat.

Felt — A thick cloth made of wool or animal fur matted together without weaving or spinning.

Finishing — Ironing and smoothing the newly completed hat.

Fulling — Thickening the hat body by adding hair to the felt and shrinking the body.

Hardening — The pressing and folding of a batt into a shape from which a hat could be made.

Hurdle — The special bench at which a bower worked.

Napping — Raising the hairy surface of the felt with a comb.

Napping Comb — A tool used for raising the nap on a newly made hat.

Planking — The repeated dipping of a hat body into hot water and rolling it on a plank.

Pouncing — Rubbing the newly finished hat with pumice, to make it smooth.

Rolling Off — Dipping the hat body in water and rolling it to mesh thoroughly together the hairs of the nap that had been added.

Runner-down Stick — The stick used to work the string down the hat body placed on a block, thus forming the crown of the hat.

Stamper — A tool used for pressing some of the water out of a newly formed hat.

Stopping — The patting of fur on the thin places of a wet hat body, with a brush.

Index